AWARENESS

AND

SENSITIVITY

exercises & techniques

By Frank J. MacHovec

The Peter Pauper Press

MOUNT VERNON • NEW YORK

4/24/84

COPYRIGHT
©
1974
BY
FRANK J. MAC HOVEC

CONTENTS

Introduction

This is a manual of self-discovery games (or exercises) to help you become more fully aware of and to better understand your own thoughts, feelings, attitudes, and values.

It's best to use this book with at least one other person, reading each exercise aloud, then doing it. The book is arranged in such a manner that skills are developed gradually, from the beginning to the end. So start at the beginning and work your way through.

Small groups of from six to twelve people provide the opportunity to interact with different personalities. Fewer than six means greater depth and more intimacy. More than twelve means greater distance; it will take more time to get acquainted and to give everyone enough time to develop awareness.

It is possible to use this book alone, but one other person makes for far better learning and understanding. A husband or wife, trusted friend, family, coworkers, classmates, club members, are all very good possibilities for setting up an awareness group.

F. J. M.

Awareness and Sensitivity

Awareness: What? Why? How?

Nobody really wants to be phony. We'd all like to be real, natural, genuine. That means being relaxed with yourself, feeling at ease, just being you. It's an *OK feeling*. When we are in that "mental space" we make lasting friendships and more intimate marriages.

Before you can understand others you must understand yourself. And the first step towards self-understanding is awareness. To get in touch with the real you, perhaps for the first time, that's the beginning. Having thus met yourself, you can decide whether to continue as you are, fully understanding what that means, — or change to whatever kind of person you want to be. Yes, you *can* change. If you don't believe that, wait until you've become more familiar with who and what you are. If you don't like what you see, whatever it is you dislike helps motivate you to change.

Change is easier once you see what you want to be, the kind of person you want to become. *Becoming* is the key word. Personality is never finished. Personal growth is an on-going, continual process, challenging, exciting, adventurous. You are being, not a being. And there's far more to you than the simple sum of the parts — no psychological test yet devised can sum you up. Your body may be worth a few dollars for its chemical components but the mind is priceless, for it is the human mind which has produced the world's great art and literature, its science and technology.

You are much more than a two-legged mammal, a creature, a subject (or an object). You are a *person*. And that's quite enough. You are delightfully imperfect, like a rough-cut diamond. Only you can really know

8

where the rough spots are, what needs to be rounded off and polished to bring yourself to the highest luster. This book has been written to help you with this self-polishing process. Through these exercises you will find strengths and weaknesses within yourself. You'll get in touch with some feelings you may not like, which you will want to change. We don't say "bad feelings" because that brings in a right-wrong black-white value judgment. Feelings are neither good nor bad, they just *are*. If you don't like them, change them. You can do this with the help of a "contract partner," a trusted friend (or even a therapist or marriage counselor) who can give you feedback as to your progress.

Before we begin, you should check yourself out about your attitude. Are you really ready to begin; receptive, interested, curious? Try to develop an attitude of quiet expectation, expecting nothing special, letting whatever comes flow naturally into and out of you. That means no preconceived notions, no "mental set" for or against yourself or the person you're working with. It might be easier for you if we give you a set of self-rules:

Stay in the here and now, how you think and feel right now, at the instant you are doing the exercises, not reciting how you felt last week or last year or any time except how you feel *now.* Otherwise you are describing the you that *was,* not the you that *is.* Tell it like it is, not like it was, may or will be.

Relax and open up. It's OK. This book avoids harmful encounter techniques that could result in hurt feelings, angry confrontations, or physical injury. Don't freeze up and stiffen; stay loose.

Commit yourself. Decide *now* to give it a try. Let it happen, whatever it is. Give it a chance. Don't push the river, let it flow.

You are free to extend yourself and fully participate or to hold back, and withdraw. Others cannot know how you think and feel unless you tell them or show them. Feel free to do so. Be free.

Don't block. Don't cut off discussion, deny what you're saying and doing, avoid facing the truth. Signs of this are idle chatter, joking, changing subjects, going quiet, lashing out defensively, getting touchy, or staying on a trivial, superficial level.

10

Give feedback. If you feel like or unlike the other person (if you "identify" with him/her) say so. Don't hide it. The other person needs this information for his/her own awareness. Don't overdo it, but respect the individual as you want to be respected. To grow you must give and get feedback. It's a 50-50 sharing. Try to be sincere and helpful, don't overkill, dump (unload your own hangups), hit and run, ridicule, or play games.

Take the risk of extending yourself, exposing your inner self. If you don't do it now, when will you do it? Help others when they take risks — they'll help you when you are in the same situation. Don't "one up" or "put down" others because they extend themselves to express real feelings or are having trouble doing so. It isn't easy. Help them. Avoiding risks is safe but it's dead end — there can be no personal growth without risk.

Hold on to insight when it comes, that "Ah hah" feeling (Eureka!), the "moment of truth." It is when you see deep inside yourself and know, really know for the first time, what's there. It's a bittersweet, happy-sad experience. Keep this insight alive by reflecting it, sharing it as fully as you can with your

11

partner, reflecting it in your own mind later from time to time, and referring to it again with your contract partner, spouse, or friend.

Tune in to your own time clock. Be aware of your own internal state of readiness. Not everyone can proceed through this book, through these exercises, at the same speed. Some people need more time to see what's happening, to fully experience it. When the apple is ripe, it falls from the tree of its own weight.

Own your thoughts and feelings. Take responsibility for what you say and do, for your thoughts and feelings. When you see what you want to do with yourself, plan your work, then work your plan. Work is the word for it. Others will help you, if you (and they) want it that way. You are free. Being free means taking responsibility for yourself. You can't always blame it on society, the church, your parents, friends, bad luck. Ultimately, when all is said and done, life is what *you* make of it, not what it made of you.

Read over these self-rules again. Tune in to them. Be a sponge, but one with sharp eyes and an understanding heart. Awareness games can be rewarding, "fun things" to do. Through them you'll see more similarities in people than dissimilarities. It's a warm feeling of sharing and helping one another.

Ground Rules

There are five very important *ground rules* which apply to the exercises which follow. Read them and discuss them *before* you begin. You may want to expand on them so everyone feels equally at ease with them.

The individual is important. You have a right to be you, a right to your own opinions and feelings. You have a right to be heard. If you are in a group, the group is stronger because you are there. If you leave, the group will be weaker. We need each other to grow. Everyone is important. People power!

The object is to become more aware of yourself, who and what you are, how you influence others, and then to see who and what other people are, how they influence you. We learn from one another. You and the other person are the lessons, the textbook.

13

You are free to speak up or listen quietly, free to participate fully or to freely decide not to take part, free to explain the reasons for what you're saying or doing and free to ask that whatever you said or did go without comment or analysis. It's OK.

It's all confidential. Nothing said or done, nothing discussed, should be repeated to anyone at any time without clearing it first with everyone who is involved. We should trust each other.

You are responsible for what happens or what isn't allowed to happen, responsible for everything you say and do and everything you refuse to say and do. It's all you. You should want to answer for it all.

If you are using this book in a group, you should read and discuss these additional ground rules:

Attendance. Only group members attend these sessions. If you want to bring someone else, clear it first with the group. The same holds true for new group members after the first session — they should be voted in or out and understand that the group's vote is final. Your regular attendance is part of your responsibility. If you miss a session the group deserves an explanation. Lateness or leaving early should also be explained.

The group leader or facilitator, elected or rotated, should not interrupt anyone or interfere in group discussion except to help someone participate, clarify, prevent someone getting hurt, or protect your right to be heard fairly. Everyone should feel safe.

No drugs or alcohol should be used during sessions. You may even want to prohibit smoking. If anyone feels it necessary to take drugs, smoke, or drink, perhaps you will want to use this for discussion — the need and what it means.

No destruction of property and no hitting one another! Your freedom ends where the other person's nose begins. The object is to learn to behave like a responsible adult, like the best *you* which you can possibly be. That shouldn't mean violence of any kind.

Dropping out. If you don't like the group experience, that's OK, too. If you want to drop out permanently, share your thoughts and feelings with the others. Explaining your reasons will be a good experience for you,

15

will give you more feedback about yourself from others, and may even put you in touch with some thoughts and feelings you missed somewhere along the way.

Warmups

The following are warmup exercises. Don't skip them; they're really important. They are arranged so that you can follow the directions and do the exercise first, before reading the explanation and reacting to it. Do the exercise, then turn the page and read what happens to most people doing the same exercise for the first time.

In these exercises and throughout this book, don't feel badly if your reaction doesn't conform with that described on the following page. Some make it, some don't. Everybody's different! There are individual differences which depend on a lot of things, your own readiness and that of your partner, how you feel at the time, the effect of certain words on you, the setting, and so on. It's OK. Nobody reacts the same way to all these exercises. Would you want them to? Wouldn't life be boring if everyone behaved exactly the same? What a drag!

EXERCISE 1: NO PERSONAL PRONOUNS

Talk with your partner, or if doing this exercise alone, speak into a tape recorder, about any subject at all *but* without using personal pronouns (I, you, we, he, she, us, them). Catch yourself or one another if you violate the rule.

Time limit: Five minutes for pairs; three minutes if alone.

EXPLANATION

Most people doing this exercise feel increasingly frustrated as the time passes. The conversation becomes cold, distant, and mechanical. It is difficult, if indeed possible, to be warmly personal or to be yourself at all.

How many times did you violate the rule — more than once? Most people "get caught" and very few can keep up the conversation without using personal pronouns. The sooner you got caught, the better. If you didn't get caught early, you probably spoke very slowly and haltingly, not in your usual conversational manner.

17

Those of us who are tuned in to people find it impossible to follow the "no personal pronoun" rule. We can't help but personalize our conversations. So that's why it's a good sign if you got caught early.

It's a good idea to make your personal communications informal, warm, and personal. Use first names whenever you can, provided it sounds and is natural. Look at people more when you talk to them (you may be surprised at how little you've done that in the past). People like to hear their first name, especially if it's used in an interested, caring way. They also like to be looked at, provided it's an accepting, friendly look.

Discuss with your partner how this exercise went for you. Do you agree with this explanation? It's OK if you don't. Maybe you'll want to discuss that, too.

EXERCISE 2: No YES-No (for pairs only)

Ask each other as many direct questions as possible, the kind of questions requiring a *yes* or *no* answer. But you are not allowed to answer with *yes* or *no*. Use any other words but not *yes* or *no*. No nodding of the head is allowed and you can't answer with such *yes-no* equivalents such as: affirmative-negative, right-wrong, or words in other languages. Catch each other every time you violate this rule.

Time limit: Three minutes.

EXPLANATION

We tend to over-use *yes* and *no*. It oversimplifies our conversation, makes it more difficult to get to know one another. For example: "Do you like hot fudge sundaes?" "Yes." But if the answer were "Very much so!" you would know far more about that person's attitude, thoughts, and feelings. Answering only *yes* or *no* is too simple, leads to rigid thinking, that there's a right and a wrong way to do things.

It is better to say *yes* and *no* followed by a sentence or two of explanation. "Yes, generally, I feel this is so." "No, I don't think we should do it that way this time and here's why . . ." Parents should always add some sentence — even a phrase — of explanation after a *yes-no* to children. It may be frustrating for the parent to do this consistently, but in time the children understand why they can

19

or cannot do what they want. "No, Johnny, we'll be having supper soon." "Yes, Johnny, Mother has time to help you finger paint now."

Discuss with your partner how this exercise went for you. Do you agree or disagree with the explanation?

EXERCISE 3: A QUICKIE!

This exercise is a "quickie." It will be over almost before it starts, so listen carefully to the instructions. Think of *one thing* you can't do and share it with your partner. If doing this exercise alone, record your statement. Next, look into your partner's eyes (or in the mirror while tape recording if you're doing this alone) and say the same thing, the same statement, but with one word changed. Instead of saying "can't" substitute the word "won't." If doing this alone, tape record yourself; play back after you've read the explanation.

Time limit: None.

EXPLANATION

This was an attitude check. If you said something like: "I can't fly like a bird," then this exercise won't be as meaningful for you, because try as you will, you *won't* fly like a bird! But if you chose everyday things like flying an airplane, skiing, swimming, sewing, baking a cake, you may learn something about your verbal and non-verbal (eye contact, gestures) behavior. And the only person who can tell you about it is your partner (or the mirror and tape recorder).

We deliberately chose something trivial which we could not do. If you really wanted to do that particular thing, though, you could find the time. It probably wasn't a life-and-death, major life problem which you chose. So, if we can detect just a little defiance — in the tone of voice, in the eyes — we can learn something about how we sound and how we look in everyday conversation. How did *you* react? Share this now with your partner. If you looked and sounded rebellious, irritated (or even flat!) in this innocent little exercise, how do you sound in everyday life reacting to more important things?

You might want to have a friend tape record you on the telephone some time, without your knowing it. In this way you can learn a great deal about how you sound and the way you speak (choice of words, speed of delivery, tone of voice, use of silences, pet words or phrases, relative warmth or coldness).

Listening Skills

Most of us hear what we are prepared to hear, what we've been conditioned to hear. Few of us hear what's actually said. Fewer still really understand the message. We live in a word world, and words mean different things to different people. What's "best" or "the right thing to do" varies from one person to another. When I explain what's right or best for me, what do you hear?

There is a basic three-step communications process you can develop which will make it very difficult to be misunderstood. It involves giving and getting feedback. Once you learn the technique, it will make communicating with others far more satisfying. It can even make disagreements more agreeable.

The three steps are: statement; reflection; clarification. It means that whenever someone makes a statement to you, you have a duty to reflect it back to him in your own

22

words. Then, the third step is for that someone to clarify as to whether or not that was
the real meaning of the statement. Over the
years, we've found that the best way to reflect
is with the opening statement: "I hear you
saying . . ." It's a neutral, inoffensive word-
ing, far less threatening than: "Do you mean
to imply . . ." or "Are you saying. . . ."

The person making the statement should add
two or three short sentences explaining the
statement so that you can better reflect back
in your own words what you heard. Likewise,
you, the reflector, should use two or three
sentences. It makes for better understanding.
Clarification can be simple ("Right on, that's
exactly what I meant") or more detailed
("Well, not exactly. What I mean is . . .").

The best way to practice this three-step process is by using sentence stems or sentence
completion items. In this way, if you have a
group of several pairs, everyone has the same
sentence. And it controls the depth of the
communication, too, for you can avoid really
personal statements ("What I really dislike
about you is . . ."). Those are better suited
for encounter or therapy groups where there

is a trained professional to moderate and advise you.

EXERCISE 4: SENTENCE COMPLETION
(pairs only)

The following is a list of sentence stems which have been used successfully with groups. Take them one at a time or shop the list. It is more effective to limit the number of sentence stems to no more than five or six. Perhaps you'll want to use one or two as warmups if your group meets regularly. You may find that group members can suggest sentences which coincide more with your own group's interests.

1. *When in a new group or among strangers I feel . . .*
2. *What I like most in people (or) what I look for and need in a friend . . .*
3. *What concerns me most about my job (or about this group) is . . .*
4. *The emotion I find most difficult to control is . . .*
5. *When I'm lonely I . . .*
6. *I'm happiest or most pleased when . . .*
7. *It would be nice if . . .*

8. *When someone needs help I . . .*
9. *Those who really know me think I am . . .*
10. *I really feel sad when . . .*
11. *What I find really funny is when . . .*
12. *What really bugs (frustrates) me is . . .*
13. *When I'm angry I . . .*
14. *When I'm happy I . . .*
15. *I really find it difficult to . . .*
16. *What really hurts my feelings is . . .*
17. *What I dislike most about myself is . . .*
18. *My greatest strength is . . .*
19. *When I'm nervous or anxious in a new situation, I usually . . .*
20. *My favorite leisure time activity is . . . What do you think that means?*
21. *When I'm rejected, I usually . . .*
22. *What I like most about myself is . . .*
23. *My greatest weakness is . . .*
24. *Breaking rules that seem arbitrary makes me feel . . .*
25. *I like to be just a follower when . . .*
26. *I will assume leadership when . . .*
27. *In groups, I feel most comfortable when the leader . . .*
28. *In groups, I really feel uncomfortable when . . .*
29. *To me, taking orders from someone . . .*

30. *When I take a good look at myself, I'd like to change . . .*
31. *Something about me I wouldn't like to change is . . .*
32. *I get rebellious, irritable, annoyed, when . . .*
33. *In crowds I feel . . .*
34. *When I'm alone I feel . . .*
35. *I make myself miserable by . . .*
36. *Right now I'm feeling . . .*

EXERCISE 5: LISTENING TRIADS

After you've tried a few of the paired sentence completions in Exercise 4, you can enlarge the experience to a group of three. We call such a group a *triad* (two is a *dyad*). Determine who is A, B, and C. A and B interact and C does nothing but watch and listen. After the three-step process (statement, reflection, clarification), C comments as to how A and B communicated. For the next sentence stem, have B and C interact while A observes. Next, C and A interact and B observes. And so on. Use selected sentences from Exercise 4.

You might try opening and closing each of your awareness sessions (even if there are but two of you) with: "Right now I feel . . ." In this way, others have a brief idea of where you are and how you feel, at the beginning and at the end of the session. If you meet for more than an hour, use this same sentence stem once or twice during the session. It enables you to vent feelings in an unstructured, uncontrolled way.

Fun Things

There are some "fun things" which can be used when the time is right to lighten moods or to end one kind of exercise and begin another. Here are a few:

EXERCISE 6: WILD IDEA

No reflection or clarification should be done for this exercise. If I gave you all the money you needed, all the time off you required, to do something you've never done before, a wild idea, a crazy idea, what would you do? Focus on this, think about it for one minute. At the end of one minute I'll call "time" and you can share your wild idea with your partner or group. You don't have to explain your idea unless you want to.

EXERCISE 7: MARTIAN DICTIONARY

Think of your full (no nicknames) first name spelled backwards (Frank becomes Knarf). This is a word in the Martian language. You will have to say it aloud, define it in one sentence, then use it in a sentence. You have one minute to think about it. When I call "time" share word and meaning with the group.

EXERCISE 8: HAPPY RECENT MEMORY

Close your eyes. Think of a happy recent memory, something that happened to you within the last week or month, something that made you happy. Focus on that, whatever it was. After one minute I'll ask you to open your eyes and share this happy memory with your partner (or group).

EXERCISE 9: HAPPY CHILDHOOD MEMORY

Close your eyes. Think back to your early childhood years. You could have been seven or ten, the age doesn't matter. Think of something you did that made you feel very happy. Focus on that, whatever it was. After one minute I'll ask you to open your eyes and share with the group.

The exercises up to this point are sufficient

in most cases to "turn on" individuals and groups. People feel relaxed, at ease, more willing to communicate in a soft, low-key way. They are better able to extend themselves to others, to assume the risk of reaching out to others. They are learning that the greater the risk (rejection or hurt feelings), the greater the reward (deep personal satisfaction, feeling really good about yourself and the other person, the *up* feeling or *high*).

Perception

What do you see? What's there, or what you want to see? Just as you are conditioned to hear what you want to hear, you also look for what you have learned *should* be there. Many of us look for and often find what we expect to find. If you're programmed for trouble, you'll find trouble just about everywhere. It is very important, then, to check yourself out as to what you see.

EXERCISE 10: ROOM CHECK

Close your eyes and keep them closed until I tell you to open them again. *(See that all have done so).* This is a perception check, a quiz

29

about this room. Answer aloud if you feel sure that you're correct.

What is the color of the rug (or floor)? Walls? How many doors in this room? What kind and how many light fixtures? What kind of ceiling? Number of windows? Color of draperies? What color is my shirt (dress)? Hair? Eyes? What color is the chair in which you are sitting? (Fit the question to the room; improvise your own questions).

EXERCISE 11: STAGED INCIDENT

If you're leading a group arrange with a stooge to have him/her arrive a little late and ask a particular question word for word which the two of you have pre-arranged. At an appropriate time during the session, refer to that incident. Ask the group to try to remember the conversation between you and the stooge. You might wish to have the stooge leave the room and ask the group to describe his/her clothing as well.

EXERCISE 12: THE RUMOR MILL

Closely related to our perception is the way we pass on information about some real event or situation. As the story goes from one person to another, it is altered a little (or a lot!) with each retelling. Use one of the following rumors, or make up your own of about equal length. Type it on a 3x5 index card or type or write it on a piece of paper. The group should be seated in a circle. Hand the message to the person on your right, instructing him/her to whisper the message into the ear of the person in the next chair. The written or typed message is then handed back to you and you place it face down in front of the person to your left, the last person who will hear the rumor. Meanwhile, the rumor is passed from one person to the next until it ends with the person before whom the written message has been placed. That person states aloud the rumor. You then read the actual message or have the same person read it. Here are three sample rumors to choose from:

RUMOR A. *A school bus, heading south, turned right at the intersection when a red sports car, heading north, turned left into the same intersection. When they saw they were turning into the same street they both honked their horns but continued to turn without slowing down. The sports car seemed to pick up speed just before the crash, although the school bus driver had plenty of time to see the red sports car coming.*

RUMOR B. *Something interesting happened in the Emergency Room at the local hospital yesterday. The head nurse was arguing with an interne when the police brought in a man injured in a fight. When the nurse on duty tried to get the head nurse's attention, the head nurse turned on her and really gave her a hard time. The patient is in intensive care now. I wonder what will happen next?*

RUMOR C. *A truck was stopped in the left hand lane of the highway. It was foggy and visibility wasn't very good. A station wagon with a woman and five kids crashed into the truck but at very low speed. By the time the police came, the truck driver had taken care of the lady and the kids, disengaged the car's bumper, and made repairs to his truck. The police wrote tickets for both drivers.*

Everyone hears rumors. What is the best way to handle them? Whenever you hear a rumor that involves you and some other person, get in touch with that other person as soon as you can and check out the information. If you are not involved in the rumor, check it out with both other parties involved. If someone begins to tell you gossip, scandal, or some secret information about another person, ask if the rumor-teller has checked it out with the person involved. If this hasn't been done, say something friendly but firm, like: "I don't want to hear it unless you've checked it out with him first." A good way to stop rumors is not to pass them. An even better way is not to listen to them, one instance where it's a good policy *not* to hear what's being said.

EXERCISE 13: HIDDEN AGENDA

This is a way to sharpen your awareness and perception about what's going on around you. Type five 3x5 index cards with the instructions which follow. Five (three will do if the group is small) volunteers role-play strictly according to the instructions. No one but the actor/actress sees the instructions, and they don't show the cards to one another. The audience tries to judge what the instruction cards say by the volunteers' behavior. Stop after five minutes, and every few minutes thereafter, until each volunteer's behavior has been spotted. If the audience guess is correct, the volunteer reads the card aloud. If incorrect, the role-play continues. The group decides on some topic of interest, not too simple, nor so neutral as to be boring and uninteresting.

DISAGREER. *Disagree with everyone and everything. Deny any statement, including these instructions. Your favorite expressions: "No . . . ridiculous . . . you gotta be kidding . . . no way . . . absolutely not . . . that just won't work . . . that's stupid."*

AGREER. *Agree with everyone and everything. Agree with anyone's statement as to these instructions. Your favorite expressions: "Yes . . . that's reasonable . . . sounds good . . . I agree . . . I respect your opinion . . . you know more about it than I do."*

SNOB. *You're the smartest person here. Put down everyone. They're stupid. Your favorite expressions: "I figured you'd say that . . . not at all surprising . . . people like you think that way . . . I don't expect much from this group (or from you) . . . whenever you're ready we can continue . . . you really don't know what you're saying."*

SUPER-ANALYST. *Go off on tangents. Deliberately mislead. Nit-pick. Split hairs. Overanalyze. Your favorite expressions: "That is not the only way to look at it . . . surely there must be more to it than this . . . reminds me of a case I once read . . . what is the truth . . . what are we really doing here . . . I'm not so sure; something's missing."*

IMPATIENT-FRUSTRATED. *You have better things to do, more important things. You're very busy and want to bring everything to a quick conclusion. Fidget, sigh, squirm. Your favorite expressions: "We're not getting anywhere . . . can't we get a decision now . . . can't we move faster . . . is there no end to these meetings . . . I gotta go."*

After this exercise, discuss how typical or a-typical the behaviors were. Good actors do well. Sometimes, the card magically matches the volunteer's own personality. Discuss this, too, if it does not invade privacy or threaten anyone (remember the freedom rule).

EXERCISE 14: WEIRD SNACK

Buy a can of squid, rattlesnake, dried cater-pillars, octopus, something unusual, some-thing most people wouldn't buy regularly and few people would eat in their normal diet. Read the label to the group. Have someone open the can to prove there are no gimmicks and the food is what is described on the label. Provide toothpicks or have the volunteer who opened the can spear some of the tasty morsels so it is easy to pick them up and eat them. Pass the can around and encourage group members to eat or refrain from eating (freedom rule).

EXPLANATION

What we eat is part of our conditioning. We eat what we have learned is best for us to eat. There are dramatic differences in food and eating habits throughout the world. Locusts, grubs, rats, dogs, snakes, raw fish, even fresh warm blood are not only accepted by some peoples in various parts of the world, but are even considered delicacies. Discuss the influence of culture on our behavior.

Another aspect of this exercise is an appreciation for individual differences. If you don't like this particular food, why criticize the next person for trying it or even for liking it? Would you want to be criticized for a similar habit or preference? Discuss parallels with the generation gap, hippies, police, other countries, drug and alcohol addiction and dependence, etc.

EXERCISE 15: FAMOUS PERSON

Have each person write the name of a famous person he admires. The paper with the name is held, folded, in the person's hand. Go around the circle and have each person make a brief statement about the personality and habits of the famous person but without giving the name. After one round the group questions one person at a time for five minutes each. If no one guesses the famous person in this time, the famous person is identified and the group moves on to the next person. This exercise sharpens awareness and perception and enables you to apply the "I hear you saying" reflection technique.

Self Awareness

EXERCISE 16: PERSONALITY POLARITY

Take your "title" (teacher, bank teller) and think of an adjective which describes the kind of person you try to be in that title (*loving* wife, *helpful* teacher, *efficient* bank teller). Write these two words down and code them ROLE 1. Now think of the opposite descriptive word (*indifferent* wife, *uncaring* teacher, *incompetent* bank teller) and write these words down as your ROLE 2. The words should be your own. They need not be exact opposites according to a thesaurus or dictionary but *according to you*.

Now determine who is A and who is B in your pair. With a stopwatch, follow a *strict* role play in which you enact ROLE 1 and then ROLE 2 according to the following schedule. It is very important that you *become* ROLE 1 and ROLE 2. Say: "I am a loving wife and that means . . ." or "I am an indifferent wife and that means . . ." Do *not* say: "A loving wife is one who . . ." If doing this exercise alone, use a timer or watch the sweep-second hand of a watch or clock and respond aloud.

Partner A, Role 1 ....60 seconds
Partner B, Role 1 ....60 seconds
Partner A, Role 2 ....60 seconds
Partner B, Role 2 ....60 seconds
Partner A, Role 1 ....40 seconds
Partner A, Role 2 ....40 seconds
Partner B, Role 1 ....40 seconds
Partner B, Role 2 ....40 seconds
Partner A, Role 1 sum-up ....20 seconds
Partner A, Role 2 sum-up ....20 seconds
Partner B, Role 1 sum-up ....20 seconds
Partner B, Role 2 sum-up ....20 seconds

EXPLANATION

As this exercise continues, the sharp black-and-white difference, the polarity between your ideal and its opposite tends to get clouded, fuzzy, obscure. If you were subjected to enough stress you would probably revert back to your opposite quality. Imagine yourself with the same responsibilities but with less time, less sleep, and more problems.

This exercise brings you face to face with yourself as a human being. You are not superman/woman. There is a very definite limit to your abilities and strength. If the stress is poured on, something's got to give, and that something is *you*. Discuss this aspect of personality with your partner. If alone, reflect on it.

EXERCISE 17: FIVE DEMANDS

Sitting upright in a chair, write down five demands you make of yourself, five things you keep expecting of yourself. If you can't think of five within a reasonable time, three or four will be enough. When you have completed the list, stand up and look down at the chair. You are *top dog* making your demands of *bottom dog* or *underdog*. Make the first demand aloud. Then, sit down and answer the first demand. Stand again and make the second demand. Sit and answer the second demand. Proceed in this way through your list of demands.

EXPLANATION

Now, having made and answered the demands, close your eyes and imagine that the great judge Solomon heard the case. Imagine him weighing the evidence. What is his decision? Which side won and by what vote? Many of us are our own worst taskmaster, our own worst enemy. We're too hard on ourselves. Top dog is always on top. We seldom give ourselves a break. Maybe this exercise has been the first time you got the chance to answer top dog. Maybe this time he/she lost. Discuss this with your partner. If alone, reflect on this.

EXERCISE 18: METAPHORS

Without taking too much time (no more than 30 seconds), what would you choose to be if you had to be: An animal or bird? A plant? Any object or thing? Furniture or household furnishing? An automobile? A food? A book? Another person? A nation? A region, landform, kind of countryside? A color? A symbol or coat of arms?

EXPLANATION

While one or two of these things can be dismissed, there should be a pattern to all your choices. From this pattern you can get an impression of yourself, of how you're thinking and feeling, of your basic personality pattern. Share your impressions with a partner if you can. If doing this alone, look over your list and see what you can learn about yourself.

EXERCISE 19: FAVORITE THINGS

Limiting yourself to no more than 30 seconds for each item, write down your *favorite:* TV show and TV star; Movie and movie star; Hobby or leisure-time activity; Book; Kind of restaurant; Song or musical selection; Style and color of clothing; Famous person; Automobile; Living person; Vacation spot; Style of house.

EXPLANATION

"Show me your friends," Emerson said, "and I'll show you your true self." Listing your favorite things is a way of describing yourself. Your favorite things *are* your friends, in a way. Look over your list. What would you think of a person responding the way you did? What does it tell you about yourself? Discuss this with your partner or reflect on it.

EXERCISE 20: DESCRIBE YOURSELF!

You have exactly three minutes to describe yourself to your partner (or into your tape recorder) *without* referring to name, age, sex, occupation, race, religion, or national origin. If working with a partner, reverse after three minutes. If you run out of steam before three minutes, sit silently until the time is up.

EXPLANATION

The only thing you could do in this exercise was describe *yourself* — the real, human side. Many people have great difficulty with this exercise. If you did, too, relax. You're in good company. It was Socrates who said: "Know thyself." Two tiny words but possibly the heaviest in any language. In fact, there's a whole science committed to exploring that two-word sentence: psychology. How do you feel about *you* after this exercise? Share your feelings with your partner. If alone, reflect on the exercise and what it tells you about yourself.

EXERCISE 21: I'VE GOT A SECRET

Write one sentence or short paragraph, unsigned, describing a thought, feeling, attitude, you haven't shared with the group, or perhaps with anyone, or something you are afraid to say or do. If doing this in a group, use the same kind of pens or pencils and the same paper to ensure privacy. Collect papers and after mixing them up, read each one aloud and have group react to them. Discuss what kinds of things people tend to keep secret, what kinds of things were reported in this exercise.

EXERCISE 22: EFFIGY

Draw a picture of someone you dislike. Dispose of it any way you want to. No discussion, just do it. This exercise vents hostility and aggression. Some people are quite imaginative in the way they dispose of the picture. Others do it quickly, with feeling. Discuss how effective or ineffective this technique was for you.

EXERCISE 23: ME — REAL ME

Write down how you think others view you (the group if you're doing this exercise in a group). Then write down, in a second column, what you're really like.

EXPLANATION

Read the second column first, then the first column. The group responds to each "pair" (each item in both columns). Discuss.

EXERCISE 24: FIRST IMPRESSION

This exercise is best done after group members feel at ease with one another, or at or near the end of a group session. Individuals volunteer their first impressions of one another. Proceed in sequence, one person at a time, asking first for volunteers.

EXERCISE 25: RESOLUTIONS

Think about, discuss if you like, but decide on some specific question, area of interest, trait within yourself, attitude, thought, or feeling you want to bring up in the group session. Share this with someone in the group, or with your partner if you are working in pairs. It is your duty to help your partner with his/her "thing" as it is his/her duty to help you with yours.

EXERCISE 26: CONTRACT PARTNER

If you have an attitude, habit, or trait you want to change within yourself, it is helpful to "contract" with someone who will help you. It is called a contract because the other person gets something in return. It is an equal sharing, equal caring 50-50 deal in which you give to get. In most cases, this means giving feedback to another person about something that person is trying to do in exchange for feedback from the other person about something *you* want to do. It is important for you to choose the contract partner (assume the responsibility) and negotiate the contract together (assuming the risk).

Contracts are very helpful for married couples, close friends, families, on the job, in organizations. Contract partners or "change agents" provide input, feedback, positive reinforcement, encouragement, an interested third person, a mirror, and a source of suggestion, advice, ego support, and comfort when needed. The best contracts are between

45

people who care about and accept one another.

EXERCISE 27: NEXT OF KIN

This one's "heavy." Don't do it until you've worked through most if not all of the preceding exercises and feel that you have definitely made progress with your own self awareness.

Write a brief note (no more than one page both sides) to your next of kin, imagining that you will die within the hour and that this is your last message to anyone. To whom would you write it? What would you say? The letters should be destroyed as soon as everyone has finished but not until volunteers share how they feel. If anyone wants to read his note aloud, he may, but no one has to do so — as always, the freedom rule applies. Even if all but one chooses to read, the group should realize the right of the one individual not to share in the reading.

This exercise puts you in touch with "final things." For many, doing this exercise and the next one has been the moment of truth, contact with ultimate reality. Life is short and we are here but a short time, never to return. Now is the time to decide what we can do with the remaining time. Today *is* the first day of the rest of your life!

EXERCISE 28: OBITUARY

Write your own obituary, what you imagine a newspaper obituary would say about you. Include when you died (now or any year in the future), cause of death, who was there, who survived you, what you were doing at the time (career-wise and the immediate moment).

What were your last words? What would be your final comment or message to the world? Your epitaph?

Each person should read aloud his/her obituary, final words, message, and epitaph. While the freedom rule applies, this particular exercise is really effective and can be a deeply meaningful personal growth experience when shared with others.

Sharing with Others

EXERCISE 29: HELP ME! (pairs only)

One partner lies flat on his/her back while the other stands alongside, about even with

47

the reclining partner's waist. The partner lying down needs help in getting up and asks the standing partner to help him/her. That's all there is to it! Once the reclining partner has asked for help, gotten it, and is standing, the other partner then lies down in the same manner and the situation is reversed.

EXPLANATION

All you had to do was to simply ask your partner for help in getting up. But the way we ask! Men have great difficulty asking women for help. Sometimes, on vacation, they'll get good and lost before they'll stop at the friendly service station to ask directions. Know anybody like that? How was it with you, in this exercise when you were doing the asking? Was there an awkward childish: "Uh . . . look, I uh . . . need some help to get up"? Some peculiar smiles? Sense of humor as a defense, to make it easier? Why is that? Many of us have great difficulty just asking for help, yet it's one of the simplest little sentences in the language: "Would you please help me to get up?" How was it with you? Discuss.

EXERCISE 30: TRUST WALK (pairs only)

This is one of the most popular and most

effective of all group techniques for building trust and sharing. It is best done in a fairly large room, with few obstacles and a clear pathway around the room.

Pairs line up against one wall, facing in one direction in pairs (two files). One file (like all those closest to the wall) close their eyes on a given signal and let the sighted partner lead them once around the room. After one revolution around the room, the situation is reversed and the inside file is led, eyes closed, around the room.

A good technique to use is the old "promenade dance" method, the sighted partner holding his/her hand up, palm down, and the blind one placing his/her hand on top, fingers on the top of the wrist of the sighted partner. In this way, changes in direction can be signalled (slowing, stopping, turning right or left). A variation is for the blind partner to firmly grasp the sighted one's arm just above the elbow.

As each pair proceeds around the room, the sighted partner should bring the blind one's free hand to objects in order to sense how they feel and try to identify them without see-

49

ing them (wall, windows, draperies, table-tops, ashtrays, books). The sighted partner confirms the identification as the blind partner makes guesses.

This exercise deprives you of a sense, sight. It puts you in touch with other senses and feelings (the room seems larger, the feel of carpet or tiled floor). It also requires that you trust another person to lead you around the room, thus bringing you closer to him/her. You have to loosen up and let go to make the walk without stumbling, falling, or bumping into obstacles. You also tune in to the touch, even the tone of voice, of the sighted partner.

Discuss your feelings after completing the trust walk. Did the two of you have the same feelings? Did you lead or follow differently? How did it feel to be entirely dependent on another person? Did objects feel different to you "blind" than when you can see them? Share this experience with your partner and another couple (group of four).

EXERCISE 31: SECRET THOUGHTS

In small groups (4-6) or in the whole group if there are fewer than twelve, anonymously complete these statements:

50

What I expect from this group is . . .

It would really help me in this group if . . .

What I hope most of all about this group is . . .

What I'm most afraid of in this group is . . .

What would prevent me from sharing with the whole group is . . .

Right now I feel . . .

Write these sentence beginnings on a chalk-board or poster paper. Read each person's responses. Discuss similarities, differences, how fears and suspicions can be overcome, how shared goals and expectations can best be realized. Each person then shares how he/she feels about what is happening. Observe the freedom rule if anyone wants to "pass" without making a statement or reaction.

EXERCISE 32: APPEASE-ATTACK

In small groups (4-6) or in the whole group if fewer than twelve, carefully time for two minutes each:

APPEASE: Everyone agrees with everything and everyone as a group member says nice things about each other and the group experience.

ATTACK: Everyone disagrees with everything and everyone as a group member criticizes the group experience and each other.

Discuss feelings involved in these two exercises. Did anyone feel "phony" in the first or "threatened and nervous" in the second? Share how easy it is to "hook" hurt feelings or "cop out" and keep conversations superficial.

EXERCISE 33: EGO BOOST

Draw names to determine who goes first, second, etc. as each group member tells the group his/her strengths for exactly two minutes. The group responds for exactly three minutes for each person, telling the group member what they consider to be his or her strengths. When everyone has been processed, rotate around the room with: "How I feel right now."

EXERCISE 34: THREE BIGGEST PROBLEMS

Everyone writes, with similar pens or pencils on the same sized paper, what each considers to be his/her three biggest problems. The *unsigned* notes are folded the same way, collected, thoroughly mixed together, then read one at a time. Tabulate and group similar feelings or statements, noting them on a chalkboard or poster paper. Discuss similarities, dissimilarities. What does this illustrate about the group? Its members? Discuss.

EXERCISE 35: FOUR THINGS

Each person writes four things he/she would like the group to know about him/her. Exchange lists with partners. The partner reads the list back to the author, assuming the identity of the author. The author corrects or changes the list to make certain the four things are understood, clear and exactly as intended. One at a time, each person introduces his/her partner to the group, standing behind him/her with one hand on his/her shoulder, the other holding the list. The introduction is done in the first person: "My name is Frank and here are four things I'd like you to know about me . . ." The partner assumes the identity of the author. The author then reciprocates, assuming the identity of the partner. This can be a very moving experience and it may be best not to discuss it further. If it has been meaningful, allow two minutes for the partners to do or say whatever seems appropriate. If the group is at ease and ready to share openly, discuss how everyone felt while being introduced.

EXERCISE 36: BALANCE SHEET

Draw names to determine who goes first, second, etc. One at a time, each person is on the "hot seat." The group describes his/her strengths and weaknesses, but no negative trait can be described without first listing a positive trait. Every group member need not volunteer to make statements about others, but everyone should agree to be on the "hot seat." If anyone refuses this exercise should not be done (the freedom rule). Discuss how it felt to describe someone's traits (to judge), to hear about your own (being judged), feelings that linger afterward. Did anyone speak up more than others? Anyone remain silent? How did they feel? How did others feel about their reactions?

EXERCISE 37: NON-VERBAL COMMUNICATION

The group divides in half, forming two columns facing one another. Men should be on one side, women on the other. No one but

the leader speaks. At the leader's signal, partners approach from opposite (diagonal)
ends, a pair at a time, approaching between
the two columns, meeting in the center, in
full view of everyone, waiting for the leader's
instructions. The leader says: "Hello." The
pair communicates in whatever way they feel
appropriate but without speaking. Still standing there, the leader then says "I like you,"
and again, the pair does whatever they feel is
fitting, non-verbally. The leader says "Good-
bye" and the pair communicates this feeling.
This is done for each pair, until everyone has
participated. Group members who do not
wish to take part in this exercise may sit on
the sidelines and watch. When finished, discuss feelings during and after the exercise.

EXERCISE 38: PEOPLE MACHINE

Small groups (4-6) go to separate rooms or
to different corners of the room, taking thirty
minutes to create a "people machine," complete with sound and motion, using the group
members (people acting as gears, wheels,
moving parts, etc.). Each machine is then
demonstrated. This is an "up trip" which can
be used effectively to lighten the mood of the

group, or as a closing exercise. This exercise can also be used to analyze group dynamics (who contributed the most, the least, who dominated, who motivated the group, who was peacemaker?). Discuss how everyone felt in his role as the specific "machine part."

EXERCISE 39: CREATE A STORY

The whole group volunteers any ten nouns, then any ten adjectives. Each set of words is written horizontally (not in columns) on poster paper or a chalkboard. Small groups (3-6), create an original story using all the words. Any word can be used more than once, but every word must be used at least once. Other words are added (verbs, pronouns, etc.) without restriction. When the groups have finished, one member from each group reads the story. This exercise is an "up trip" which can be used to add humor to the group process or it can be analyzed for a better understanding of group dynamics. To analyze have each small group discuss who contributed most, least, who led, who took notes and became recorder (how, why?), who chaired the group? How was everyone's behavior received? How do the group members feel after hearing the other stories? How do they feel about their own personal participation or lack of it?

EXERCISE 40: TEN COMMANDMENTS

This exercise begins individually, with each group member composing his/her own ten commandments, imagining that it is his/her duty to reformulate the ten commandments to bring them up to date and make them more meaningful for future civilizations. When everyone has completed the commandments, pair off and synthesize ten commandments from the pooled twenty (two persons with ten each). When this has been done, two pairs join to synthesize ten from the revised ten of each pair. If the group is large enough, have two quads join to synthesize ten commandments from the quads' revised sets of ten. Discuss whose commandments remain after all the deliberation. Who lost the most? Is everyone satisfied with the ten commandments which emerge? What does this teach us about group process? Any parallels in passing legislation, influencing people, getting things done, changing society or its values?

Exercise 41: Survival Words

This exercise begins individually, with each group member composing a list of ten words absolutely essential for survival. Each member imagines that his/her mission is to form a colony on another planet, where it will be impossible to have a vocabulary of more than ten words. What should these ten basic words be? When each person has a list of ten words, pair off and synthesize ten from the pooled twenty. Join pairs and synthesize again. If the group is large enough, join sub-groups and synthesize once more. Write the ten words which finally remain on poster paper or on a chalkboard. Whose words survived the negotiations? Who lost all his/her words? How does everyone feel about the final list? Discuss the process.

Exercise 42: Space Ship

In small groups (3-6), have each group imagine that it is the crew of a space ship far from earth. It has been determined that there is no way the ship can return to earth unless it is lightened by at least 100 lbs. Computers have analyzed the situation and there is no way the ship can make it unless it is lightened.

Food, water, fuel, equipment, have all been checked and everything possible has been jettisoned. The group has thirty minutes to submit the name of the crew member to be sacrificed. The "execution" will be painless and will be done in the command ship, the mission commander taking full responsibility for all final details. Each group reports how it arrived at its decision. After the report, discuss how the victim feels, how the survivors feel, if the groups can see any other way of determining the expendable crew member other than the way they agreed upon. Were there serious differences of opinions? Hard or hurt feelings? Did anyone dominate? Anyone emerge as a leader? Sum up feelings by rotating through each crew with: "How I'm feeling right now . . ." Discuss further, if appropriate.

EXERCISE 43: NATION'S FINEST

Each small group (4-6), takes thirty minutes to create a 60-second TV commercial "selling" the group as a unit — its strengths, assets, virtues, superiority, as if competing for the title: "The world's finest people." Each group then makes its presentation. Discuss: who contributed most, least, who came up with the best ideas or central theme, who was "on camera" most of the time? Share what this exercise teaches about behavior in groups. Did it help draw group members together or separate them?

EXERCISE 44: ELECTION

In small groups (4-6) or in the whole group if fewer than twelve, vote for the group member who would make the best: Boss; Political leader; Close and trusted friend; Son/Daughter; Husband/Wife; Person to trust with an important mission.

Tabulate the results. List candidates on chalkboard or on poster paper, combining group choices (there should be more than one candidate, then, for each office), and have an election in the whole group. If the group agrees, small groups can appoint campaign managers and prepare a 60-second TV commercial for each candidate before the election for each office. Use secret ballots. Discuss feelings throughout: the winning and losing candidate's feelings before-during-after the election. Discuss the decision-making process.

Exercise 45: What's in a Name?

Group members say the first name of each person in the group in a whisper, a shout, with varying feelings (coaxing, angry, belittling, sensual). Rotate from one person to another through the group until everyone has had his/her name called. After each name calling, the named person shares how he/she felt — which way was most pleasing? Most objectionable? Most neutral? What does this tell us about the effect of tone of voice, gestures, and eye contact, on communications?

Exercise 46: Indian Wrestling

To vent hostility between two group members, have them sit facing one another in a comfortable position at a firmly situated sturdy table. Right elbows rest on the tabletop, forearms upright, hands clasped. Left hands are clenched and resting on the lap. At the leader's signal ("1-2-3") each person tries to push the other's right hand down to the tabletop. Elbows must remain in contact with the table throughout, the left hand cannot be used for leverage on the chair or table, and both feet must remain flat on the floor throughout. This exercise is used if and when two group members become angry, have need to vent hostility, and when not doing so would hamper group progress or cause the two to take the anger home, displacing it on others.